101 Limericks About Public Speaking

By
Paul Benson
&
Glen Ford

With
Illustrations By Aputik Gardiner

Published by
Training NOW
Mississauga, Canada

101 Limericks About Public Speaking

Published by TrainingNOW Press, Mississauga, Ontario
http://www.TrainingNOW.ca

ISBN 978-0-9867885-0-5

To order additional copies of this title, contact your local bookstore, order online from Amazon.com, order online from http://www.TrainingNOW.ca , or call 1-866-518-5247.

Cover Graphic: Aputik
Interior Illustrations: Aputik

101 Limericks
About
Public Speaking

1. Introduction

The importance of humour is plain
When you're trying to explain the arcane
It's still just as true
When trying to break through
Boredom, disinterest, and pain.

Humour is a very useful tool in any trainer's bag of tricks. It can entertain, relax, or break up a long information session. More importantly, it can also make a needed point clearly and succinctly with much more impact than any other means of explanation.

In the case of public speaking it has another function. It can help overcome fear. After all, we laugh the most at things we fear. Public speaking has long been known as a major cause of fear. In fact it is the number one fear – much higher even than the fear of death!

But humour is a temperamental mistress. It takes timing, practice and an ability to communicate a sense of the absurd. The experience of the blown punch line is one to which any professional comedian can relate. And even if the timing is right there is no guarantee that the audience will find it funny. Is it any wonder that so many of us simply can't carry it off?

Instead we need to rely on others to make the point for us. Which leads us to often fruitless searches through many a month of Sunday funnies. And whispered prayers to the gods of comedy that our audience will both get the point and find the result funny.

During our courses on public speaking, facilitation and train the trainer we've found that limericks work the best. They're long enough to make their point clearly and low enough that even if the punch line misses the mark, people enjoy them. The problem is finding just the right limerick about public speaking and then creating a visual that complements the message. And so we created this book.

We hope that you'll enjoy our collection of limericks about public speaking. We've included limericks illustrating as many of the points about public speaking as we could think of. And then we matched them with the artwork of Aputik and put it all together in a book form for your enjoyment and ease of browsing. We've also put it into a format that allows you to copy the limerick and the artwork into your own overheads.

Enjoy, keep speaking and keep smiling!

Paul Benson & Glen Ford
www.TrainingNOW.ca

2. Rewards & Results

When people refer to communications today they mean the internet. It's true; the internet has meant a fundamental shift in patterns of communication. Friends are more likely to be found on the other side of the world at the end of an internet chat than on their porch or in the house next door.

Despite this change in speed and distance there is one skill that remains untouched: The ability to speak – clearly, concisely and with purpose – to other people. In fact, the rewards to those who can speak well have increased. There are more opportunities to speak in a public forum and correspondingly, there is an increased need for individuals to speak well in front of an audience This is a skill that will never become out of style.

Building Pride & Confidence

A savvy old man from Keswick
Said "Speaking is surely my stick.
I get very proud,
When the applause is loud.
This is the best life to pick"

A sprightly old lady from Bow
Said "I still love to go
Out onto the stage
Where, improving with age,
I deliver an inspiring show"

A popular speaker from Kentucky
Said "I've always been very lucky
But more luck appears
When I conquer my fears
And try something new and plucky"

There was a young lady of Rheims
Said "Nobody values my schemes
If I speak with more skill,
They'd all get a thrill
And help me pursue my dreams"

Changing Others' Perceptions of You

A reclusive techie from Guelph
Said "It's time I got off the shelf
If I learn to speak
I'll look less of a geek
And that's got to be good for the self"

A great speaker who walked with a cane
Showed audiences what they gain
When they don't see
Just disability
But all that someone can attain.

Changing Others' Perceptions of You

There was an old man from Chert
Who said, "To be an expert,
You just need to speak
And within a week
You'll be at the top of the heap – or just dirt!"

When leaving the convention hall
Some may be untouched at all
But others may find
A new frame of mind
As a result of how you enthral.

Making A Difference

A very young lass from Milton
Said "When speaking at the Hilton
My ideas will surprise
And some folks may surmise
That their world is a tilt'n"

There was a young man of Dundee
Who said "I'll be all I can be
I work hard and aspire
To take people higher
And reduce mediocrity"

Making A Difference

A lady from Trincomalee
Said "I give my speeches for free
I get satisfaction
When people take action
And that's reward enough for me"

A wise lady from old Maastricht
Said "This is the life I've picked
Through the medium of speech
I inform and I teach,
And hopefully resolve conflict"

Making A Difference

A Buddhist from the Far East
Said "A good speech is just like a feast
It delights the senses
Breaks down your defences
And calms the inner beast"

If the late king Richard the Third
Had been more adroit with a word
Would he have died in his bed,
Not pole axed in the head?
Or am I just being absurd?

Making Money

To avoid cold calling each day
There is, simply put, just one way
Have your customers call
Nothing else, that's all
Through public speaking you'll make your pay.

If you really hope to sell
There's no choice, you must speak well.
To start wealth creation
Just speak 'round the nation
On whatever it is rings your bell.

3. Fear of Public Speaking

A recent survey placed the fear of public speaking as number one – well ahead of the fear of death itself. Even famous actors have admitted to a fear of speaking in public.

Unfortunately, there is no real reason to fear public speaking. Your audience is on your side. They want you to succeed – if only to justify the time they've spent listening to you.

Why unfortunately? If there was a real reason it could be easily identified and overcome. Since there is none, we are forced to overcome an unreasoning fear. And humour (even in the form of limericks) is one way we can examine, share, and thus learn to overcome the fear.

The Effects of Fear

There once was a young man of Neath
Who suffered from chattering teeth,
Whenever he spoke,
His courage just broke,
And he left a small mess beneath.

The Effects of Fear

When giving a speech in Leeds
An experienced speaker concedes
It wasn't his best,
When he fell on the breast
Of an elderly lady in tweeds.

There once was a student from Stoke
Whose teeth chattered whenever he spoke
His heart missed a beat
And he bounced on his feet
Until he had finished his joke.

There was a young man from Bavaria
Said "I find few things scarier
Than speaking at length
When I have little strength
In that particular area"

A speaker from Rio Grande
Said "I find it very handy
To quell my fears
With one or two beers
And maybe a very large brandy"

Good Solutions

There was a young fellow from Delf,
Who said, "Just be yourself!
The audience will support.
You don't need any port
Or other strong drink from the shelf"

When your stomach starts to feel tight
And your body screams "flee or fight"
Turn all that stress
into effectiveness
And your speaking will turn out alright.

Good Solutions

A determined speaker from Stroud
Said "I'm fearful of speaking out loud,
But I concentrate hard
And, here's my trump card,
I'm really the best and darn proud"

I don't mean to seem mostly dense
But the key seems to be confidence
If you speak with pride
They'll go for the ride
And you'll gain a grateful audience.

Good Solutions

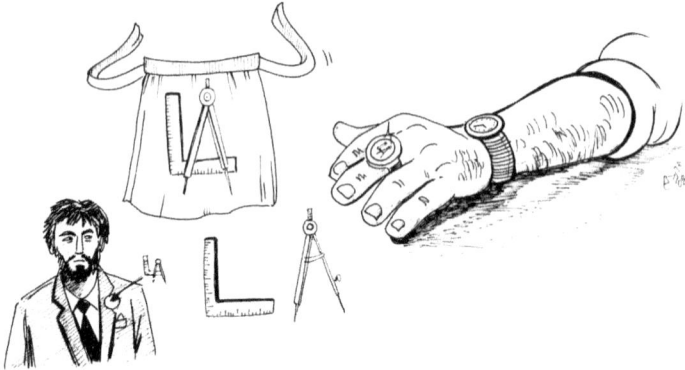

Oh many, so many the reasons
For joining a group like the Masons
The rituals they do
Are perfect for you
To practice speaking in all seasons.

Consider Toastmasters too
They'll share all their secrets with you
And give you the chance
To polish and enhance
The speaking skills you accrue.

On the Relative Importance of Fear

Don't worry that you won't speak well,
There's a trick that old fogeys tell.
The audience it seems,
Just like in your dreams,
Is actually wishing you well.

Worst Case Scenario

The auditorium looks immense
And you're feeling incredibly dense
Fear has you frozen
You gave up supposin'
That you speaking here makes any sense

But you haul up what courage you can
And try to follow the plan
To speak clearly and loud
And be heard by the crowd
But that quickly goes down the pan

When you get to the dreadful end
Of a talk that would surely send
Your supporters to sleep
Your reputation to the heap
Then all will applaud, or pretend.

" THE SPEAKER You don't wANT To Be ARound "

4. Bad Habits

We all believe that we have more than our fair share of in-built bad habits when it comes to public speaking. However, as we found out when we tried to write these limericks, it's simply not true.

Most bad habits are the result of nervousness – they're nervous ticks, not underlying faults. By studying our own speaking we bring our habits out into the open, and find that very few of us have more than one (or often any) real bad habits. And since nervous habits reinforce our nervousness, eliminating the few we have helps to reduce our fear of public speaking.

While giving a speech in Madrid,
I can't believe all that he did.
He mumbled and stumbled,
and fumbled and bumbled
And all agreed - it was horrid.

Nervous Ticks

There was a teacher from San Martin
Who was well known for snortin'
He sounded like a pig,
And blew off his wig,
At least it was better than fartin'.

A man who gave talks at resorts
Frequently got out of sorts
While he was complaining
My interest was waning
But worse were his ***awful snorts.

Nervous Ticks

When giving speeches in front of a group
He showed all the symptoms of croup
His nose would be running,
He'd cough 'til becoming
Unable to do more than stoop.

A speaker with a terrible runny nose
Said "most of you might suppose
It would be quite piffling
To control this sniffling
But it's a bad cold, and I'm in its throes"

A speaker from Puerto Vallarta
Was a terrible, noisy farter
He tried to contain it
But couldn't restrain it
And everyone felt like a martyr!

A speaker from Birmingham
Persistently drums with his thumb
When he isn't drumming,
He insists on humming
How on earth can I make him keep mum?

Vocal Habits

There once was a politician from Kent
Whose voice it came and it went
But that was okay
He was heard to say
At least my ethics aren't bent.

There once was a speaker from Stoke
Who stuttered whenever he spoke
But he tried so hard
He won their regard
And their support for him slowly awoke.

Vocal Habits

There once was a man from Rhone,
Who only spoke in monotone,
Most people slept,
While others, they wept,
Whenever he called on the phone.

A man from Bangor, Maine
Showed everyone his total disdain
The crowd dissipated
As everyone hated
To listen to such a big pain.

Poor Body Language

A speaker from Wyndham Hill
Stayed unnaturally still
The audience were scared
With the way that he stared
And some thought he'd taken a pill.

A speaker who lived in New Delhi
Tended to get rather smelly
To cure his B.O.
He bathed in cocoa
Now he smells just like Ghirardelli.

Other Bad Habits

A politician called Robert McNabb
Once delivered an uncalled-for jab
He was quite naïve
And failed to perceive
That he was the one it would stab.

A visitor from Woking
Said "I hate being around people smoking
I'll sit and I'll listen
Until my eyes glisten
But I just feel that I'm choking"

5. Good Habits

While we may not have bad habits as public speakers we do have one very bad tendency – we fail to cultivate and follow good habits. Good habits are those actions which take a so-so speech and turn it into a memorable speech. Following them consistently will make an average speaker into a great speaker. But as teachers of public speaking we don't want to harp on those habits. Here are a few limericks which may just help remind you how to pull the right strings.

There was a young woman from Staines
Who waxed lyrical about drains
The subject is boring,
Most folks start snoring
And someone invariably complains.

Keep Your Audience in Mind

When speaking to colleagues take care
To understand what they can bear
What's fun in your brain
May make interest wane
And cause them to leave in despair.

There once was a very old devil
Who said, "I always speak on their level.
To get a quick bargain
Don't bother with the noggin,
Just appeal to the heart with a revel!"

Keep Your Audience in Mind

When Stephen Hawking talks quantum physics
He doesn't need to use tricks
His appearance belies
His intellectual size
As he brings life to complex academics.

There was a man from South Bend
Who no-one could comprehend
The points he was making
Had most heads shaking
And very few stayed to the end.

Engage Your Audience

When Steve Jobs gets onto the stage
He does many things to engage
He points, walks, and talks;
and the audience squawks
His presentations are always the rage.

There was a young man from Purdue
Who said "It's so easy to do,
I hook their attention
And without dissension
They're ready to learn something new"

Engage Your Audience

When speaking you're making a pitch
So you'd better make your speech rich
In interesting tales
And sufficient details
So it goes off without a hitch.

There once was a woman from Rome
Who said "I'm adventuresome
I love to pursue
All experiences new
And then bring them right back home"

Engage Your Audience

A young man from Tokyo
Said "I want to see faces aglow
When I tell a tale
That removes a veil
And gives people more to know"

There was a young man from Calais
Said "It's not just what I say
But how I show you
How it affects what you do
That might just make your day"

Be Positive

A panellist from Tangiers
Had people almost in tears
He argued and fought
Against every good thought
And left the room to jeers.

When, as speakers we try to aim higher
We hope that we might inspire
Others to reach
For their ultimate niche
And then we may light a new fire.

Be Honest With Your Audience

An elderly man from Greece
Talked about finding peace
But his biker jacket
And drug-selling racket
Drew attention from the police.

A teacher from the West End
Tried to be everyone's friend
His attempts to be nice
Didn't break the ice
And all hated him in the end.

Be Honest With Your Audience

When speaking in front of a crowd
It's not enough just to be loud
But speak with conviction
And practise good diction
You'll find your audience wowed!

There was an old man who would squawk,
"If you want people to accept your talk,
To get people to believe it
You really need to live it
Or they'll get up and leave -- they'll walk!"

There's A Reason They're Called Visuals

There was a young lady from Bellepointe,
Who fell in love with PowerPoint
Since it was all the rage,
She filled page after page
While her audience screamed "She's missed the point!"

There's A Reason They're Called Visuals

A map helps me pick out the places
That I use in most of these cases
First those from round here,
Then some that are queer
And then I'm off to the races.

There's A Reason They're Called Visuals

Use images rather than words
And your thoughts will fly like birds
To the words that you say
More attention they'll pay
And your audience will love what they've heard.

There's A Reason They're Called Visuals

A speaker from distant parts
Showed his audience beautiful charts
"They tell so much more
Than words which might bore
You can tell I'm a fan of the Arts"

There's A Reason They're Called Visuals

An instructor from Gretna Green
Said "From all that I've seen
If I can just show
How it should go
Things quickly become routine"

Edit, Edit, Edit

To ensure that your speech is a hit
Get rid of any unnecessary bit
If you don't follow this rule
You'll look like a fool
And people will say it was...disappointing.

Edit, Edit, Edit

There was a young man from The Hague
Who couldn't resist being vague
When asked to explain
He tried – but in vain
And was avoided like the plague.

There once was a lady from Lands End
A copy of her speech she would send
To her agent by post
Though it was grandiose
And, under the load, he would bend.

Edit, Edit, Edit

Here are some tricks that I use
I use simple words not abstruse
A dictionary of rhyme
I use all the time
To cut down on words I abuse.

There was a young man from Glen Abbey
Said "I usually tend to be gabby
But for speeches I choose
To keep focus and lose
Anything that will make my speech shabby"

Edit, Edit, Edit

This speech was starting to drag
And I knew that was a red flag
So I cut it right back
To keep it on track
And now it is done, I can brag.

An entrepreneur from Glace Bay
Said "I didn't come here to play
So speak most concisely
And wrap it up nicely
And we'll all have a very good day"

Edit, Edit, Edit

A woman from Surrey once said
"Speaking too much is widespread
I give you the scoop,
Without all that poop
I hope you like my way instead"

Edit, Edit, Edit

Some speeches refuse to end
But here's what I contend
The very best plan
Is to speak with élan
And never to overextend.

Edit, Edit, Edit

When giving a very long talk
You know some listeners will balk
So try to be brief
And give some relief
And fewer of them will walk.

Check Your Facts

There once was a young man from Bradure
Who never sounded particularly sure
His facts were confused
And logic he abused
It was bad – but his intention was pure.

Practice, Practice, Practice

A foolish young man from Falaise Ittuit
Believed it was better to wing it
Than practice all day
What he had to say
Until his boss rated him a right twit.

A good speech doesn't come right
'Til you've practiced it night after night
Refine and make clear
All that you hold dear
And then it will be a delight.

Practice, Practice, Practice

A presenter who just read each slide
From the audience got a rough ride
"We expected more knowledge
From a prestigious college
Not someone who never even tried"

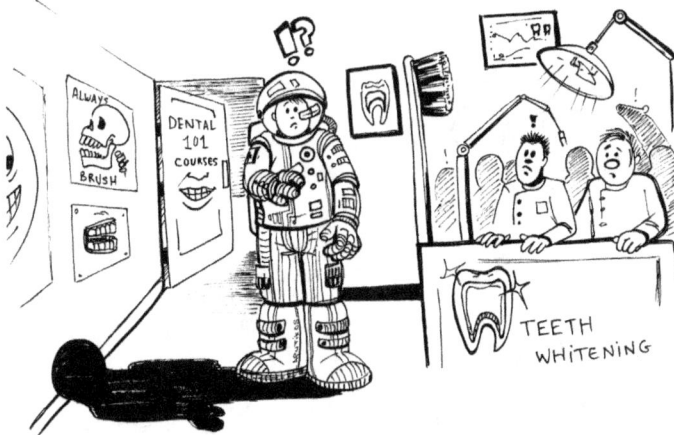

A young man from Liverpool
Said "I've never felt more of a fool
I was in the wrong room
Gave my talk on Khartoum
When they expected dental school"

Prepare In Advance

A young man from Dorking
Said "Nothing is working
The projector is dead
I'll have nothing instead
My preparation I've been shirking"

If you wish to gain confidence,
Speak with a rhythmic cadence,
Use a poem or two
To ensure that you
Are perceived as both smart and intense.

Study Others To Improve

There was a young man from Glen Eden
Said "One thing I won't be needing
Is tips on what's right
When I talk tonight"
He really had no chance of succeeding!

There was a young speaker named Hector
Who said, " Why watch a mere actor
I don't need to learn
I've got talent to burn"
His audience just walked out the faster.

Study Others To Improve

When trying to become the best
Pay attention to all of the rest
Some ideas may fail
They may seem to flail
But understand they're still on the quest.

An old professor from Margate,
Started lectures ten minutes late.
He said "Why worry?
I'll just make them hurry.
Even though that's what they hate"

Be On Time – Start & Finish

There once was a speaker from Danong
Who always went on far too long.
His audience said,
"We're ready for bed.
His sense of time is just wrong"

There was a speaker from Lime
Who always started on time
"If you want to entertain"
He would always maintain,
"You need to respect their dime"

Be On Time – Start & Finish

There once was a young speaker from Thyme,
Who always finished on time,
His competition they jeered,
But his audience they cheered,
And he celebrated with a lager and lime.

There once was a man from Tobruk
Who revelled in every second he took
"He always entertains"
His audience maintains
"Gets us laughing with just a look"

Add Energy

A sensitive man from Trieste
Often got quite depressed
When folks didn't care
For all he would share
But he always gave it his best.

A recruiter from NASA Aerospace
Just bounced all over the place
As he talked of the joys
Of teaching girls and boys
About the glories of outer space.

Add Energy

A young presenter called Doug
Had all the energy of a slug
He could barely speak
- More of a squeak
Until he had his coffee mug.

At a medical conference, a young Swede
Completely failed to take heed
Of why they were there
At a medical fair
When he tried to sell them some weed.

6. A Speaker's Tools

One mistake that no craftsman can afford is not to know how to use their tools to best advantage. And a speaker's tools are many … from their voice, to their body language, to the visuals, and even to the room setup itself. In fact, many of the most important of the good habits – practice, practice, practice and preparation, for example – are focused on learning to use the speaker's tools well. So we've included a number of limericks which help to illustrate some good practices for using those tools well.

Sometimes it's the room that's the pits
Taking away all the glitz
If there's no way to cure
All the things that are poor
Then just do the best it permits.

The Room

Next time check rooms in advance
And take a very strong stance
This just will not do,
It's not fair to you
But you should never leave it to chance.

Slide transitions some think are sublime
But I think they just waste my time
I'd be six slides ahead
But you decided instead
To carry on this pantomime.

Microphones

Few use a microphone well
The others are easy to tell
They bang and they tap
Like a thunderclap
For the audience it's like entering hell.

Should the mike be placed on the chest?
Some people think that's the best
But the audience may hear
Your lunch and that beer
Rumbling under your vest.

Microphones

What about a boom by the lips?
It works fine unless it slips
You'll look like Celine
Or a cyborg machine
Resulting in more than a few quips.

When conferencing on the 'net
I say it's the best it can get
No one can see
If I'm having my tea
'Cause I don't have video yet.

Video-Conferencing

Now I'm presenting on video
I have to put on a good show
My screen just shows green
But my video machine
Makes me seem on a beach in Bordeaux.

7. 101 + Just Two More

Congratulations on making it to the end!
We hope you enjoyed our little collection of limericks.
Please feel free to use them shamelessly in your own training
courses – we do. In fact this is the first in a series of 101
Limericks books – one for each of the course groups we train in.

Why?

Firstly, because just like you we want and need to use humour in
our courses (or humor if you prefer). And we're not professional
comedians (or even gifted amateurs, if you believe our wives and
families).

And secondly, as you may have noticed there are actually more
than 101 limericks in this book. The blasted things are habit
forming!

Of course, we simply claim that, just as in our courses, we want to give our readers just a little more than we promised ….

We wanted to give more than expected
With this set of rhymes we collected
When we were done
We had more than 101
Even after some were rejected.

So enjoy and share these with your friends, colleagues and clients … just remember to blame them on us. After all we went to a lot of work to create these things Hey, trying to keep a straight face is harder than it looks! …

In creating a book of limericks
We needed to develop a set of tricks
Without them in mind
We feared we would find
We looked like a real couple of hicks.

Enjoy & Great Speaking …

Paul Benson

Glen Ford

Aputik ◁>∩ᵇ

Mississauga, Ontario, Canada
2008.07.15

www.ingramcontent.com/pod-product-compliance
Lightning Source LLC
LaVergne TN
LVHW022318080426
835509LV00036B/2634